The BEASTS of BETHLEHEM

Also by X. J. Kennedy

BRATS

FRESH BRATS

THE FORGETFUL WISHING WELL:
   Poems for Young People

GHASTLIES, GOOPS & PINCUSHIONS

THE KITE THAT BRAVED OLD ORCHARD BEACH:
   Year-Round Poems for Young People

(*Margaret K. McElderry Books*)

The BEASTS of BETHLEHEM

verse by X. J. Kennedy
drawings by Michael McCurdy

MARGARET K. McELDERRY BOOKS
New York
Maxwell Macmillan Canada · Toronto
Maxwell Macmillan International · New York · Oxford · Singapore · Sydney

In earlier versions, some of these poems appeared in *Glamour,* in *Wildlife's Holiday Album* (National Wildlife Federation), and in Myra Cohn Livingston's anthology *Poems of Christmas* (Atheneum / Margaret K. McElderry Books).

Text copyright © 1992 by X. J. Kennedy
Illustrations copyright © 1992 by Michael McCurdy

Margaret K. McElderry Books
Macmillan Publishing Company
866 Third Avenue, New York, NY 10022

Maxwell Macmillan Canada, Inc.
1200 Eglinton Avenue East, Suite 200
Don Mills, Ontario M3C 3N1

Macmillan Publishing Company is part of the
Maxwell Communication Group of Companies.

First edition
Printed and bound in Hong Kong by Toppan Printing Co., (H.K.) Ltd.
10   9   8   7   6   5   4   3   2   1
The text of this book is set in Meridien.
The drawings are rendered in scratchboard and colored pencils.

Library of Congress Cataloging-in-Publication Data
Kennedy, X. J. The beasts of Bethlehem / verse by X. J. Kennedy ; drawings by Michael McCurdy. — 1st ed.   p.   cm.
Summary: Presents nineteen poems, each in the voice of a creature that was present in the stable at the time of Christ's birth.
ISBN 0-689-50561-2
1. Jesus Christ—Nativity—Juvenile poetry.   2. Children's poetry, American.   3. Christian poetry, American.   4. Christmas—Juvenile poetry.   5. Animals—Juvenile poetry.   [1. Jesus Christ—Nativity—Poetry.   2. Animals—Poetry.   3. Christmas—Poetry.   4. American poetry.]   I. McCurdy, Michael, ill.   II. Title.
PS3521.E563B4   1992   811'.54—dc20   91-38417

For Naomi

—X. J. K.

CONTENTS

The BEASTS of BETHLEHEM

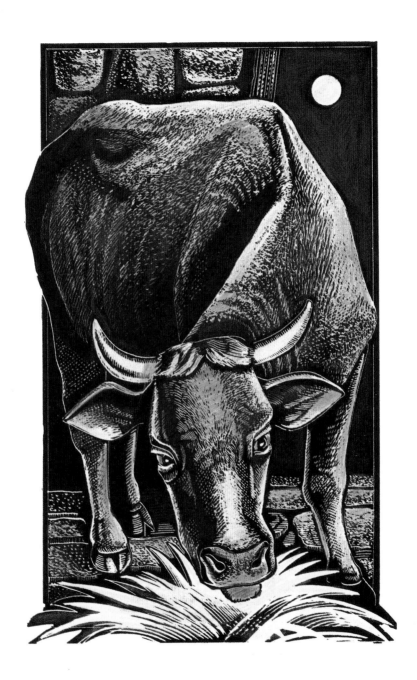

COW

He came to conquer death
And yet His hands are small.

To warm Him in his stall,
I breathe my clover breath.

OWL

Being no wiser, men believe me wise
Not for my hoot, but for my full-moon eyes.

They are my mask. I see through not a soul
But only mice to fill my beak and bowl.

Perched in the eaves, I let my dreams congeal.
Who are these kings? Why do the oxen kneel?

HORSE

On Christmas Eve, the night unique,
They say we beasts find tongues to speak,

Yet at this crib I am so stirred
That, staring, I can say no word.

CAMEL

Stepping painstakingly
Over dry desert sands,
Making my way with a side-to-side swing,
Led by a star to a stable in Bethlehem,
On my back's mountain I
Carry a king.

Gaspar, my rider, his
Throat parched from journeying,
Kneels by the manger now, one of the first
Shepherds and kings to lay eyes on the Little One—
Who'd dream a Child could bring
End to long thirst?

SHEEP

My wool in clumps like moss,
My diamond eyes agleam,
I bleat my sheepish praise,
But no one hears.
                    Who cares
What sheep think of the Lamb of God?

No matter. I'm content
To bask in lantern light.
I must not doze and dream.

The flocks that shepherds watched
Watch over Him tonight.

MOUSE

Permit me, friends, my evening meal,
These few small crumbs of bread I steal.

I mean no harm. Remember that.
Why do you shriek and call your cat?

The Infant's mother fears no mouse
But lets me scamper round her house

Of manger hay. Beside this Child,
Let man and mouse be reconciled.

CAT

Mouse, without me, there'd be no end of mice.
You'd carry off the loaf to the last slice.

I wait to pounce, a trap set for release.
Between us, how can there be lasting peace?

And yet—the Babe is born. Tonight I pause.
Play with my whiskers. Scamper past my claws.

SNAIL

High on an oaken beam
I'm stuck fast. Here I dream.

My wobbling eyes though dim
Behold the light of Him.

For bed I never lack—
I bear it on my back,

A chamber snug and dry.
Had Joseph done as I,

The Child in Mary's womb
Had found an inn with room.

HEN

How costly, how immense
The gifts some people bring!
Sweet-smelling frankincense,
Whole flowing bowls of gold—
But me, I'm not a king.

Mine is a common gift
Fresh from the chicken-run—
One warm brown-speckled egg
Laid at His feet. I beg,
Accept it, Little One.

HAWK

Before Christ, yesterday,
　　From clouds I dived, gave chase,
And fed. But in this place
　　Of peace I shall not prey

On living things. Those six
　　Young hares ripped from their burrow
Were lovely, though. Tomorrow,
　　Old plump hen, watch your chicks.

ANT

To come here I made haste
    Not on account of her
And Him, but for a taste
    Of a spilled drop of myrrh.

Feelers atwitch, I gaze.
    Down drops my varnished jaw.
I scurry in amaze
    About the spun-gold straw.

HUMMINGBIRD

Stowaway in the fold
Of a black Wise Man's cloak,
I rode from Mozambique
Having endured fierce cold,
Wind, rain, and billowing sand—
Yet I have come thus far
To settle in His hand
And whir, His personal star.

BAT

Hanging head down, I hear Him cry,
Drawing His first breath, see Him try

His human fingers. Oxen keep
Watch over Him. I fall asleep

And dream that in a glow of gold
That Child whose birth had been foretold

Whispers to me, "Dear Bat, come do
That task which God assigns to you."

And so, obedient, I rouse
To hunt mosquitoes in the mows.

MOSQUITO

Who but a blind bat swaddled in his wings
Could dream that I might bite the King of Kings?

GOAT

I am a beast of beard and twisted horn
That some think wicked. Now that Christ is born,

You who upon a scapegoat lay your blame,
To whom *old goat* is an insulting name,

Come, let us kneel beside the barley cart
That He may choose which are the pure in heart.

WORM

Through the deep midnight of the ground
I move, immune to light and sound,

Mere mouth with neither ears nor eyes
Beneath the stall in which He lies.

My lot in life is but to toil
At chewing tunnels through packed soil.

A human babe is born divine?
Well, what concern is that of mine?

OX

An ark unsettled from its Ararat,
I rise, move to and fro,
One weak eye on the Child.

So old I drool. My underwater eyes
Blink in distrust: Can He be infinite
Who lies like daisies on a heap of straw?

Smoke circles in the stall
Where shag-haired Joseph, old a man
As I am ox, stands guard
On the mother as she rests
Among the easy beasts,
The old ox amovering along.

BEETLE

Lowliest of the low, I live among
The floorboards moist with fresh-dropped cattle dung.

Men see me, bring a boot down, and I die—
Can any beast be more despised than I?

Yet when I lift my dull eyes to the sight
Of Christ the Child, they blaze with blessèd light.

DONKEY

The only steed poor Joseph could afford,
I carried her who held the unborn Lord.

Feeble and old, heart slowing to a stop,
Hardly the strength to lift my feet and clop,

I had gone but a hundred yards, no more,
Under the sacred burden that I bore

When April's birdsongs filled my startled ears
And suddenly the tons of all my years

Rolled from me, and it seemed that Mary mild
Weighed no more than a leaf though great with Child,

And I, for whom a new world would begin,
Stepped lightly toward my stable at the inn.